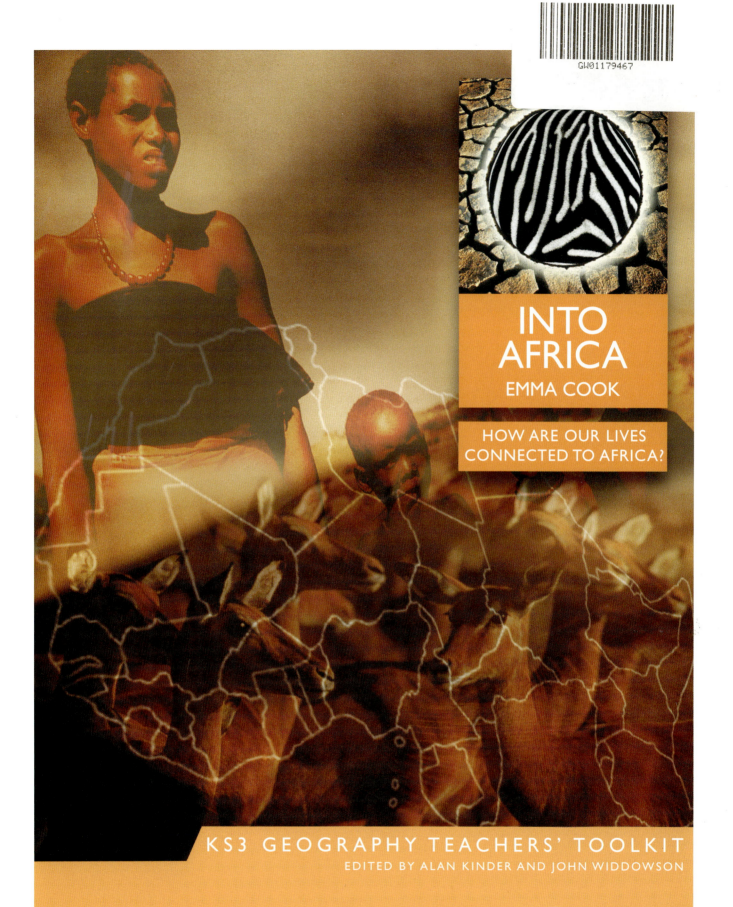

INTO AFRICA
EMMA COOK

HOW ARE OUR LIVES CONNECTED TO AFRICA?

KS3 GEOGRAPHY TEACHERS' TOOLKIT
EDITED BY ALAN KINDER AND JOHN WIDDOWSON

Geographical Association

Acknowledgements

Thanks to Dr Jennifer Hill of UWE for supplying the information for Lesson 2.

Thanks to Sarah Maude and Margaret Mackintosh for supplying photographs and information about Kibera and Kicoshep.

Thanks to Kevin Cook for general information and support during this project.

© Emma Cook, 2008

This book is copyright under the Berne Convention. All rights are reserved. Apart from any fair dealing for the purpose of private study, research, criticism or review, as permitted under the Copyright, Designs and Patents Act 1988, no part of this publication may be reproduced, stored in a retrieval system, or transmitted in any form or by any means, electronic, electrical, chemical, mechanical, optical, photocopying, recording or otherwise, without the prior written permission of the copyright owner. Enquiries should be addressed to the Geographical Association. The author has licensed the Geographical Association to allow members to reproduce material for their own internal school/departmental use, provided that the author holds the copyright. The views expressed in this publication are those of the author and do not necessarily represent those of the Geographical Association.

ISBN 978 1 84377 202 6
First published 2008
Impression number 10 9 8 7 6 5 4 3 2 1
Year 2011 2010 2009

Published by the Geographical Association, 160 Solly Street, Sheffield S1 4BF.
Website: www.geography.org.uk
E-mail: info@geography.org.uk
The Geographical Association is a registered charity: no 313129

The GA would be happy to hear from other potential authors who have ideas for geography books. You may contact the Publications Officer via the GA at the address above.

Edited by Andrew Shackleton
Designed by Bryan Ledgard
Printed and bound in China through Colorcraft Ltd, Hong Kong

KS3 GEOGRAPHY TEACHERS' TOOLKIT

CONTENTS

Editors' Preface	4
Chapter 1: About Into Africa	5
Chapter 2: Medium-term plan	12
Chapter 3: Lesson plans	16
Chapter 4: Glossary	36
Chapter 5: Links for further ideas and resources	37
Chapter 6: Assessment framework	39

KS3 GEOGRAPHY TEACHERS' TOOLKIT

EDITORS' PREFACE

The *KS3 Geography Teacher's Toolkit* is designed to help teach the new key stage 3 curriculum from 2008. The series draws on the Key Concepts, Key Processes and Curriculum Opportunities in the new Programme of Study and applies these to selected parts of the Range and Content. For teachers, it provides timely guidance on meeting the challenge of creating and teaching the curriculum. Each title in the series illustrates ways of exploring a place, theme or issue of interest to young people and of geographical significance in the twenty-first century. The selection of content is carefully explained, ideas are clearly linked to the new Programme of Study and advice is provided on the use of teaching strategies to engage and challenge all learners in the classroom.

The *Toolkit* can be used in a number of ways. For busy teachers of geography, under pressure from curriculum change throughout the secondary phase, each title in this series provides a complete unit of work: a bank of ready-made lesson plans and accompanying resources. These materials can be used *directly* in the classroom, with minimal preparation. The printed resources in each book may be copied directly, but complete resources for every lesson are contained on the easy-to-navigate CD.

Toolkit materials can also be extended. Each title provides links to websites of interest and to further resources and reading, encouraging teachers and students to 'dig deeper' into their chosen places, themes and issues. Activities within each unit can be extended

into full-scale enquiries, to stretch even the highest attainers.

The *Toolkit* has also been designed to be adapted. Teaching strategies are explained throughout each book, allowing teachers to understand the 'how to' of each lesson activity. It is hoped that teachers using these materials will be encouraged to select ideas, change them to meet the needs of their own learners, and begin to use relevant teaching strategies elsewhere in their curriculum. Each title is therefore a rich source of teacher-to-teacher advice, a 'professional development' resource that can be used to inform the teaching of places, themes and issues of your own choosing.

Lastly, the series provides a template for writing new curriculum materials. Unit summaries, concept maps linked to new Key Concepts, assessment frameworks, glossaries, lesson plans and other materials are included as exemplars of rigorous curriculum planning.

By using, extending, selecting and adapting appropriate 'tools' from the *Toolkit*, teachers will gain confidence in developing their own materials and creating a high-quality curriculum suited to the needs and interests of their learners. We hope that the series will help teachers fully exploit the rich potential of the new KS3 Programme of Study.

Alan Kinder and John Widdowson, 2008.

KS3 GEOGRAPHY TEACHERS' TOOLKIT

1. ABOUT INTO AFRICA

Why teach about Africa?

Africa is a diverse continent
Africa is often, mistakenly, seen as a homogeneous land. In fact, it is extremely diverse geographically, culturally, religiously and politically. The continent is home to desert, rainforest, temperate, savannah and coastal ecosystems and the 'greatest number of animals in the world' (Reader, 2001). While this diversity and complexity presents challenges when deciding what learning should take place, with the new, less prescriptive, Programme of Study there is now greater freedom to explore a varied range of physical and human geography.

Africa highlights global inequalities
Our world contains staggering inequality, with poverty for many and prosperity for a few. This is unsustainable and morally unacceptable. Learning about Africa enables students to begin to make sense of this complex global picture and helps them to consider what it means to enjoy wealth while so many are denied the very basics. Through exploring their existing geographical imaginations of Africa, then challenging and building upon them, we can help students to gain a realistic sense of what it is like to live in Africa in comparison to the UK (see, for example, Figure 1).

Many students have connections with Africa
Studying Africa is important in our increasingly globalised world, where the movement of people has led to our classrooms becoming ethnically and culturally diverse. The 'local has become global' (Joseph, 2000). While this could lead to increased understanding and respect for difference and diversity, in reality this is not always the case. Learning about Africa, and the experiences of people living there, is a way for students to better understand their connections with Africa. Taught well, this should promote increased sensitivity and tolerance, enabling students to become good global citizens.

Learning about Africa can teach us about ourselves
'Learning about places is not just knowing about places themselves, but understanding the interdependence and connectivity of places' (Bell, 2005). It is vital to study places such as Africa in order to gain an understanding of the interdependence of places and explore our place in the world with a critical mind. Africa connects to our lives in a variety of ways: many foods we eat come from Africa, African footballers play in our football leagues, we visit Africa for our holidays, and issues of global concern, such as HIV/Aids, affect both the UK and Africa.

Figure 1: For the inhabitants of camps for internally displaced persons in civil-war-torn countries, mobile phones are the only means of communication with relatives and the outside world. Elsewhere in Africa mobile phones are as much a part of everyday life as they are in the UK.

Photo: Abbie Traylor-Smith/Panos.

KS3 GEOGRAPHY TEACHERS' TOOLKIT

How to teach about Africa

Build on students' geographical imaginations

Students come to the classroom with mental images of places that they carry around in their heads. These 'geographical imaginations' are developed from a variety of sources: from visiting places, from talking to friends and family, from classroom learning and from the media. All of these complex images combine into a multi-layered image of places, the most detailed of which is likely to be their own local area.

One learning theory, constructivism, states that 'learners construct new knowledge by building on what they already know' (Brooks and Morgan, 2006). Therefore, encouraging students to think about their own area and life experiences can be a way of 'bridging their understanding from what they already know to gain an insight into other perspectives' (Brooks and Morgan, 2006). Furthermore, students can make connections and comparisons between their own life and Africa, thus helping them to gain a global sense of place.

Avoid the temptation to oversimplify a complex world

Africa is complex and diverse. This makes teaching about Africa at key stage 3 challenging and there is a temptation to oversimplify. It is important that these complexities are not glossed over, but instead they need to be explicitly taught. This can only be achieved by abandoning the idea of teaching about the whole continent and focusing instead on a few key areas that provide a deeper insight into life in Africa in the twenty-first century.

Recognise multiple identities

A key consideration, when teaching and learning about places, is to recognise that a place can have multiple identities. Therefore, when teaching about Africa, we need to present resources and activities that help students understand that it is a continent with multiple identities and is not totally homogeneous. Using a range of different resources helps to give each student the opportunity to engage in different ways with information presented and allows for different outcomes. This is important as most students have no first-hand experience of the developing world and so need to be, where possible, taken on a 'virtual journey' so that they can gain a sense of 'what it might be like to actually experience a place without actually being there' (Taylor, 2005).

Select resources carefully

Resources need to be selected carefully in order to avoid presenting a 'partial representation of that place which may misinform young people' (Lambert, Martin and Swift, 2005). One way of presenting a range of authentic perspectives is to include oral testimonies (e.g. the Panos Institute project 'Mountain Voices'), speakers from the continent, African feature films, school links with African schools, African literature and newspapers. Experiential learning opportunities can also be valuable for helping students to empathise with African lives and enabling them to visualise places. For example, tasting food, listening to music, building shelters and touching artefacts.

Summary

In this unit, students begin to make connections between their lives and peoples' lives in Africa. They explore the key concepts of place, cultural understanding and diversity and interdependence. They investigate a range of topics and issues that are likely to be relevant to students: holidays, shopping, football, mobile phones and Comic Relief.

Prior learning

In key stage 2 and key stage 3, it is likely that students will have learnt about a locality in a developing country. Popular key stage 2 choices are India and St Lucia. Students may have developed geographical imaginations of what developing places are like. They are also likely to have carried out a detailed local area study.

Future learning

There are many ways of developing the learning that will take place in this unit. Students could learn about other places in both the developed and developing world, and make comparisons between these places and Africa. Some of the topics and issues studied in this unit could be investigated in more detail. There are many other important aspects of African human and physical geography which could also be studied.

Key learning outcomes

Most students will be able to:

- explore their geographical imaginations of the UK and Africa
- explore social, economic and environmental connections between Africa and the UK
- appreciate the differences and similarities between people, places, environments and cultures
- present and evaluate information to draw plausible conclusions
- understand and empathise with others' lives
- use atlases and maps to develop their knowledge and understanding of Africa.

Some students will not have made so much progress but will be able to:

- use atlases and maps of Africa at different scales
- recognise the connections between Africa and the UK
- present information and draw simple conclusions.

Some students will have progressed further and will be able to:

- begin to understand the significance of interdependence in change.
- present information in a variety of ways and evaluate it to draw substantial conclusions
- understand how places are changing and the implications of this change for people.

KS3 GEOGRAPHY TEACHERS' TOOLKIT

The geography behind Africa

Multiple identities of Africa

Photo: Emma Cook

'How do you hunt? How do you keep animals? How do you eat? Do you fetch wood for your fire? Do you have wells? What do children wear to school? Are their teachers like ours? Do you have Peulh (nomadic pastoralists)? Do you have black people? Are black people accepted by white people? Do you carry babies on your backs like we do?' (Questions posed by children in a Burkina Faso school, quoted in Brazier, 1995).

'It is the girls who rise first in the village of Adballah Wallo and go for water even before the sun is up. This is a fortunate village: water is nearby. All one has to do is climb a steep, sandy bank down to the river…after reaching the river, the girls fill tall, metal tubs and plastic canisters with water, help one another place them on their heads, chatting, and climb the steep incline back to the village' (Kapuscinski, 2001).

'Geographically, Africa resembles a bulging sandwich. The sole continent to span both the north and south temperate zones, it has a thick tropical core lying between one thin temperate zone in the north and another in the south. That simple geographic reality explains a great deal about Africa today' (Diamond, 2005).

Photo: Jungle Photos.

'Botswana is one of Africa's biggest economic success stories. Money from the country's diamonds has been spent wisely to give the country strong foundations for future growth. As a result, it is now described as a "middle income" rather than a "poor income" country' (Commission for Africa, 2005).

Photo: Margaret Mackintosh.

"Poverty is chronic: average incomes have remained stagnant since the mid-1970s and over this period of time Africa's small share in world trade and investment flows has got even smaller' (Lockwood, 2005).

'People living in extreme poverty can't escape from it. The cycle of poverty continues from one generation to the next. Around a sixth of the entire population of Africa south of the Sahara, more than 100 million people, are chronically poor. In Ethiopia, people who are very poor – and therefore have little in the way of food are known as "those who cook water"'(Commission for Africa, 2005).

'Most of us continue to see Africa as an object, a single, blighted place burning in the relentless heat, for others it occupies a romantic space in the imagination of child-like primitives and wild, beautiful creatures. For yet more of us it's the dark side of our minds, the impenetrable place, the unknowable mind. And yes, all of this is partially true too much of the time. But there are other Africas' (Geldof, 2005).

Photo: Jonathan Lorrison.

Photo: Eric Fichtl.

Photo: Emma Cook.

Photo: Emma Cook.

9

KS3 GEOGRAPHY TEACHERS' TOOLKIT

Concept map: Africa

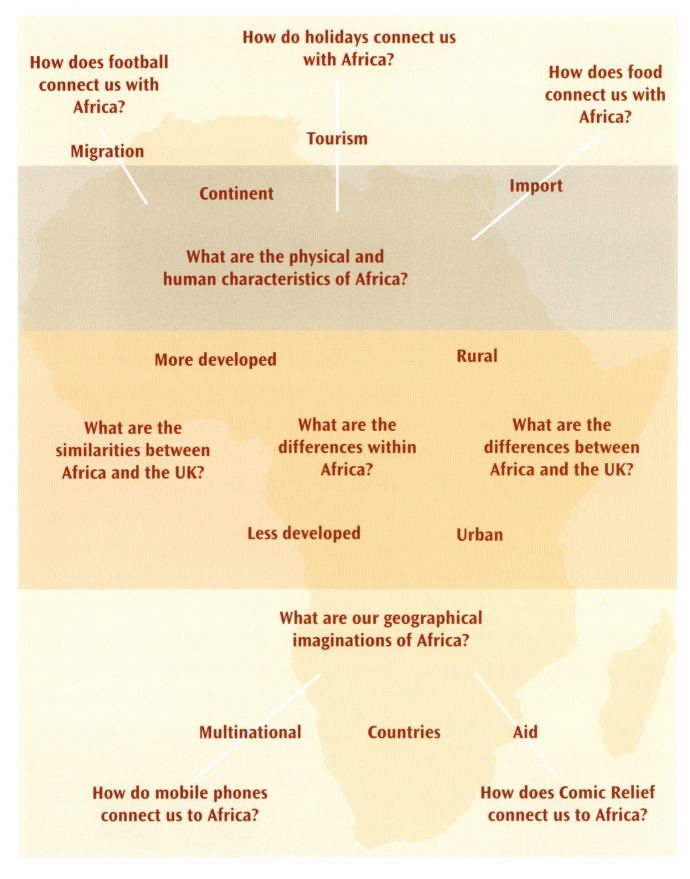

Key concepts

Interdependence Place Cultural understanding and diversity

KS3 GEOGRAPHY TEACHERS' TOOLKIT

Links to the National Curriculum Programme of Study

Key concepts

Place
- The whole unit is about the continent of Africa. It focuses on selected African countries.

Interdependence
- The unit explores social, economic and political connections between the UK and Africa.

Cultural understanding and diversity
- The unit encourages students to compare their lives to African lives and to appreciate the diversity present within the continent.

Key processes

Geographical enquiry
- Each lesson in the unit is structured around key questions that students investigate
- The data students require to carry out their enquiry is provided
- There are many opportunities for students to carry out research tasks.

Graphicacy
- Students use atlases, maps at a range of scales, photos and other geographical data.

Range and content

- The unit considers African countries and how they relate to other parts of the world, particularly the UK. Issues studied have relevance to the lives of students
- The unit is primarily about human geography.

Curriculum opportunities

- The unit uses a range of enquiry approaches
- The unit uses varied resources, including maps and visual media
- The unit examines geographical issues in the news
- The unit investigates important issues of global relevance using a range of skills, including ICT.

KS3 GEOGRAPHY TEACHERS' TOOLKIT

2: INTO AFRICA
Medium-term plan

Lesson	Key questions	Learning objectives	Teaching and learning	Resources	Assessment opportunities
1	How do holidays connect us to Africa? What are some of the physical and human characteristics of African tourist attractions?	To develop students' geographical imaginations of places in Africa To be able to use an atlas to find countries, cities and attractions in Africa	Focus on an imaginary trip around Africa to visit some of its best-known attractions Students research people who have lived, worked in or visited Africa, and share findings with the class Students imagine they are going on a trip around Africa. They complete a map exercise matching statements to dots on an Africa map Students discuss their findings	Information Sheet 1 Activity Sheet 1 Figures 2-14 from CD Atlas	Students complete the mapping exercise using an atlas Students take part in class discussion, or answer questions
2	What has been the impact of tourism on Matmata, a Tunisian settlement? How do peoples' attitudes to tourism differ?	To explore the impact of tourism on Matmata To analyse and display information in a variety of ways	Focus on investigating the impact of tourism on a village through studying maps and other data Introduce students to Matmata Students study two maps and 'spot the difference' Students read through Matmatan people's daily routines and complete two bar charts Students read through speech bubbles and complete a table outlining the impacts of tourism Feedback session	Information Sheet 2 Figures 15 and 16 from CD Video or DVD of *Star Wars* if possible Activity Sheet 2 Information Sheet 3 Activity Sheet 3 Colouring pencils	Students complete bar charts to show daily routines of people in Matmata Students complete a table outlining the advantages and disadvantages of tourists visiting Matmata
3	How does food connect us to Africa? Should we only buy British food?	To be able to collect and record information about where our food comes from To analyse and evaluate evidence to draw and justify conclusions	Focus on research to find out where our food comes from and consider whether we should buy British For homework or classroom task, students to research where our food comes from Students discuss their research findings Students consider whether we should buy British by reading through and classifying information and discussing some of the associated issues	Activity Sheet 4 (completed as homework prior to the lesson) Activity Sheet 5 Information Sheet 4	Students record information they find out about food Students complete an information sorting activity Students take part in class discussion

12

Lesson	Key questions	Learning objectives	Teaching and learning	Resources	Assessment opportunities
4	How do shopping facilities affect people's daily lives in Malawi?	To develop students' geographical imaginations of rural Africa To use maps to understand the elements of daily life in an African village	Focus on the shopping facilities found in Chinamwali village as a way of learning about peoples' lives Introduce students to Chinamwali village Students complete a map exercise to gain an idea of shopping facilities and daily lives in Chinamwali village Students consider what impacts certain events would have on people's daily lives and shopping habits and complete a table	Information Sheet 2 Figures 17-22 from CD Activity Sheet 6 Information Sheet 5 Activity Sheet 7	Students complete the map exercise based on Chinamwali village Students complete a table outlining impacts of possible changes
5	How does football connect us to Africa?	To analyse and evaluate evidence to make decisions To be able to understand and empathise with others' lives	Focus on the dilemma of a young African person whether or not to take up an offer to work as a professional footballer in Europe For homework, students research African footballers playing for British clubs Introduce students to the Ivory Coast Students read a letter from a young African asking for advice. They consider the advantages and disadvantages of African footballers leaving the Ivory Coast to work in European football. They write a letter in response Students read their letters offering advice	Information Sheet 2 Information Sheet 6 Information Sheet 7 Activity Sheet 8	Students write a letter giving advice
6	What are the likely impacts of the 2010 World Cup on South Africa?	To explore the likely impact of the 2010 World Cup on South Africa To analyse and evaluate evidence to draw and justify conclusions	Focus on the impacts of the 2010 Fifa South Africa World Cup Introduce students to South Africa Students identify the key elements and aims of the 2010 World Cup. They think of a good slogan Students carry out a card sorting activity to gain an idea of the likely	Information Sheet 2 Information Sheet 8 Activity Sheet 9 Figure 23 from CD Large pieces of	Students carry out a cost-benefit analysis justifying their decisions in pairs and with the teacher Students write about the likely impacts of the 2010 Fifa World Cup

KS3 GEOGRAPHY TEACHERS' TOOLKIT

Lesson	Key questions	Learning objectives	Teaching and learning	Resources	Assessment opportunities
			costs, benefits and problems of the hosting the 2010 World Cup Students classify cards into economic, social and environmental impacts	sugar paper Colouring pencils	
7	How do mobile phones connect us to Africa?	To analyse and evaluate evidence to draw and justify conclusions To consider how our decisions could affect people in Africa	Focus on how a person from the UK and a person from the DRC are connected by mobile phones Students look at photos of two people and consider how they are connected Introduce students to the Democratic Republic of Congo Students read seven cards that tell the story of how the two people are connected. Students discuss the main points Students investigate whether anything should be done about coltan mining by reading through different options and then completing a table	Information Sheet 2 Figures 24 and 25 from CD Information Sheet 9 Information Sheet 10 Activity Sheet 10	Students complete a table on what should be done about coltan mining
8	How have mobile phones been changing lives in Nigeria and the UK?	To understand how places are changing and the implications of this change for people To appreciate the similarities and differences between the UK and Nigeria	Focus on the ways that mobile phones are changing lives in Nigeria and the UK For homework, students complete a research task and complete a table on how mobile phones have changed people's lives in the UK Students read through information and complete a table about how mobile phones have changed people's lives in Nigeria. They complete a table to compare mobile phone use in Nigeria and the UK Students give a talk, or act a scene, to show how different things might be in ten years' time	Information Sheet 2 Figure 26 from CD Activity Sheet 11 (completed as homework prior to the lesson) Information Sheet 11	Students complete a table comparing changing mobile phone use in the UK and Nigeria
9	How does Comic Relief connect us to Africa?	To develop students' geographical imaginations of urban Africa To interpret place and space through creating a model	Focus on building a model of a shanty home as a way of empathising with a family in Kibera Introduce students to Comic Relief and Kibera, Kenya Students read a profile of David, a resident of Kibera	Information Sheet 2 Comic Relief website: (www.red noseday.com) Information Sheet 12	Students complete a scale model of David's home Students analyse aspects of David's life

KS3 GEOGRAPHY TEACHERS' TOOLKIT

Lesson	Key questions	Learning objectives	Teaching and learning	Resources	Assessment opportunities
9 cont.		of a shanty town home	They empathise with a Kibera family by making a model of David's home . They analyse their experience	Activity Sheet 12 Information Sheet 13 Card for photocopying Activity Sheet 12 Scissors and sticky tape	
10	How has Comic Relief helped to change lives in Kibera?	To analyse and evaluate evidence to draw and justify conclusions To understand how places are changing and the implications of this change for people	Focus on a Comic Relief project in Kibera, Kenya and how it is changing lives Students explore a project run by Comic Relief – the Kicoshep youth centre – through carrying out a hot-seating activity. They write a newspaper article about the project Students think of all the connections between the UK and Africa through the unit	Information Sheet 12 Information Sheet 14 Information Sheet 15	Students carry out hot-seating activity Students describe ways that Kicoshep is helping to improve lives

15

KS3 GEOGRAPHY TEACHERS' TOOLKIT

LESSON 1:
How do holidays connect us to Africa?

Key questions
- How do holidays connect us to Africa?
- What are some of the physical and human characteristics of African tourist attractions?

Key words
- tourist
- continent
- country

Resources
- Information Sheet 1
- Activity Sheet 1
- Figures 2-14 from CD
- Atlas

Learning objectives
- To develop students' geographical imagination of places in Africa (you may need to explain to students what geographical imaginations are. Tell them that they are images of places we carry around in our heads).
- To be able to use an atlas to find countries, cities and attractions in Africa.

Assessment opportunities
- Students complete the mapping exercise using an atlas
- Students take part in class discussion, or answer questions

Starter
As a homework task set earlier, ask students to find out if any of their friends or relatives have lived or worked in or visited Africa. They could ask them some of the following questions:
- Were you born in Africa? If so, where?
- Did you live in Africa? What was the place like?
- Did you work there? If so, what work did you do?
- Did you visit Africa for a holiday? If so, where did you go? What were the places like?

> A common misconception many students have is that Africa is a country. It would be helpful, right at the start, to explain that Africa is a continent. Define the words 'country' and 'continent' for students.

- Did you go to Africa on business? If so, where? What type of business was it?
- What was the weather like? What was the landscape like?
- Students could share their findings with the class.

Main teaching and learning phase
Give out Information Sheet 1, Activity Sheet 1 and an atlas to the students. The photos (Figures 3-14) could be shown to students either on an interactive whiteboard or by printing copies.

Tell students to imagine they are going on a trip around Africa visiting some of Africa's main attractions.

Students read through the statements on Information Sheet 1. To decide which statement matches which dot on the map on Activity Sheet 1, they need to pick out the key words that help them locate the place in an atlas. The country names are shown in italics and the attractions are shown in bold. Once students have matched the statements and dots, they write the attraction and the country in the boxes on Activity Sheet 1. The first one is done for students.

Students then try to match the photos (Figures 3-14) to the attractions to develop their sense of place. Figure 2 shows the answers.

Plenary/review
Conduct a class discussion.
Ask the following questions:
- Which attraction do you think you would enjoy visiting the most? Why?
- Are there any attractions you wouldn't want to visit? Why?
- Why are there few attractions in the Sahara Desert?
- Why are there few attractions in the centre of Africa?
- Which attractions are historical sites?
- What are the benefits of British tourists visiting attractions in Africa?
- Any there any problems with British tourists visiting attractions in Africa?

> Instead of conducting a class discussion, students could write down answers to the questions. This provides a further assessment opportunity.

16

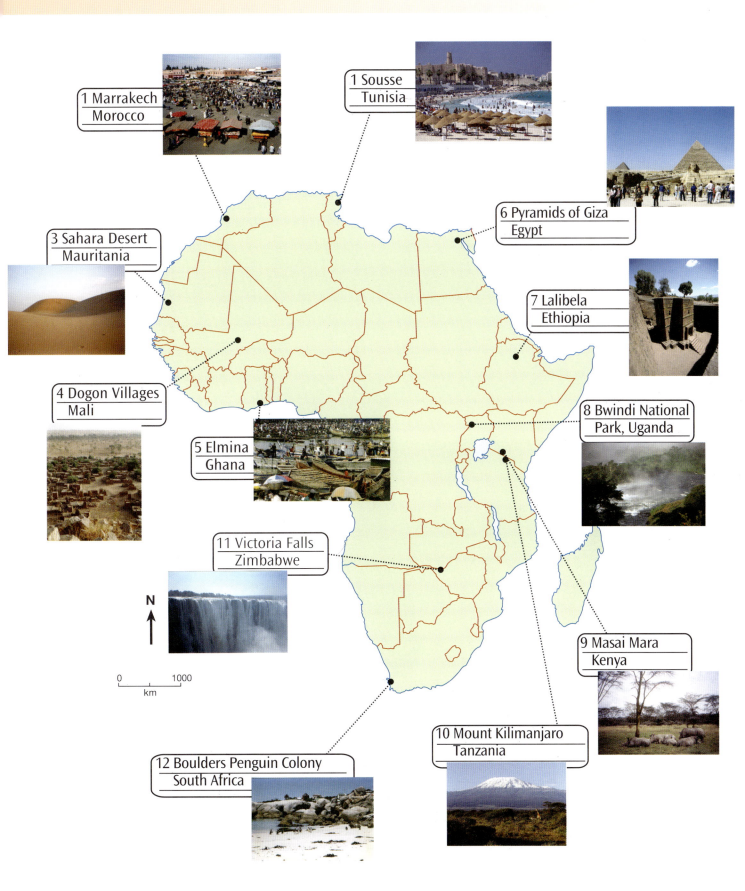

Figure 2: How do holidays connect us to Africa?

17

KS3 GEOGRAPHY TEACHERS' TOOLKIT

LESSON 2:

What has been the impact of tourism on Matmata, a Tunisian settlement?

Key questions
- What has been the impact of tourism on Matmata, a Tunisian settlement?
- How do people's attitudes to tourism differ?

Key words
- tourist
- tourism

Resources
- Information Sheet 2
- Figures 15 and 16 from CD
- Video or DVD of *Star Wars* if possible
- Activity Sheet 2
- Information Sheet 3
- Activity Sheet 3
- Colouring pencils

Learning objectives
- To explore the impact of tourism on Matmata
- To analyse and display information in a variety of ways.

Assessment opportunities
- Students complete bar charts to show daily routines of people in Matmata
- Students complete a table outlining the advantages and disadvantages of tourists visiting Matmata

The 1976 film *Star Wars* was filmed on location at the Sidi Driss Hotel in Matmata, Tunisia. The hotel is made up of traditional Berber homes carved into cavern walls which were used for the sunken desert homestead where Luke Skywalker lives. Showing students the relevant section of the film would be a good way of creating a sense of place.

Photos: Eric Fichtl.

18

LESSON 2: Information Sheet 2

The places in Africa studied in this unit

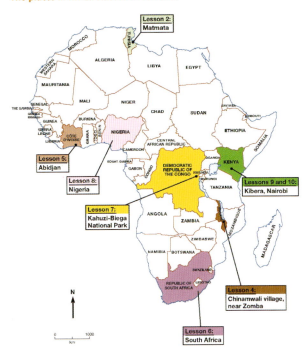

Information Sheet 2, used in several lessons in the unit, shows the location of the places studied.

Starter
Introduce students to Matmata by showing them where it is on the map of Africa (Information Sheet 2). Show an extract from *Star Wars* or show photographs of Matmata (Figures 15 and 16). Give students a copy of Activity Sheet 2 and Information Sheet 3. Students study the two maps and 'spot the difference'. They write down five differences between the maps and share these with the class after the activity.

Main teaching and learning phase
Students read through the accounts of people's daily routines in Matmata 30 years ago and today from Information Sheet 3. They use the information to complete the bar charts on Activity Sheet 2 to show what people are doing at different times of day both for a family 30 years ago and for a family today. Students label where the time is spent on the bar charts. One has been completed as an example.

> In this lesson students analyse data in the form of maps, diaries and opinions. They re-present the data as bar charts and a table. Increasingly, through key stage 3, students should be able to analyse and present data in a variety of ways.

Give out Activity Sheet 3. Students read through the speech bubbles of different people's views of how tourism has impacted on life in Matmata. They use these, and all the other information from the lesson to complete the table.

Plenary/review
Students feed back their ideas about the impact of tourism on Matmata that they recorded in the table in Activity Sheet 3. Ask the following questions:
- What are the main changes that have taken place in Matmata over the past 30 years?
- What are the advantages of tourists visiting Matmata?
- What are the disadvantages of tourists visiting Matmata?
- How different are the primary school children's futures likely to be compared to that of their parents?

Set the homework task for lesson 3. See next lesson plan for details.

Thanks to Dr Jennifer Hill of UWE for supplying the information for this lesson.

KS3 GEOGRAPHY TEACHERS' TOOLKIT

LESSON 3:
How does food connect us to Africa?

Key questions
- How does food connect us to Africa?
- Should we only buy British food?

Key word
- import

Resources
- Activity Sheet 4 (completed as homework prior to the lesson)
- Activity Sheet 5
- Information Sheet 4

Learning objectives
- To be able to collect and record information about where our food comes from
- To analyse and evaluate evidence to draw and justify conclusions.

Assessment opportunities
- Students record information they find out about food
- Students complete an information sorting activity
- Students take part in class discussion.

Prior to the lesson
Give out Activity Sheet 4 for the students to complete as a homework task (this could be also be done in class using ICT). Students research where our food comes from. The table on the left has a list of foods that often come from Africa and the list on the right contains foods that often are grown in the UK. The worksheet suggests where students can find the information.

> The worksheet is designed to give students the freedom to find out about foods they choose – they shouldn't have to complete all of the worksheet. Students could also identify products with the Fair Trade label.

Main teaching and learning phase
Students mark where the food comes from on the map on Information Sheet 4 then use Activity Sheet 4 to discuss their research findings in pairs. They could also ask whether the countries that their foods came from are the same as those found by their partner and why they think this is.

Give out Activity Sheet 5. Students read through the boxes. In one colour they underline the reasons why it is good to buy British and in another colour they underline the reasons for buying from Africa.

> Underlining reasons to buy British or buy African is an example of a DART (Directed Activity Related to Text). It can help to focus students' reading and make them think as they read.

Plenary/review
Conduct a class discussion. Ask students the following questions:
- Why would they buy British food?
- Why would they buy food from Africa?
- Should we only buy British food?
- Should we buy more food from Africa?

Finally, as a class, ask the students to vote on whether they would buy only British foods. Ask students to justify their decision.

KS3 GEOGRAPHY TEACHERS' TOOLKIT

Photo: Bryan Ledgard

Should we buy British?

- If we don't buy British foods, British farmers are in danger of losing their farms and their livelihoods.

- Importing foods from Africa supports African farmers who rely on selling crops to survive.

- Importing food from Africa allows us to enjoy a wide range of foods that we can't grow in this country. We can also eat foods all year round, e.g. we can eat strawberries in winter.

- Buying food that comes from Africa means that this food has been shipped or flown thousands of miles to get to us. The fuel used to ship or fly these foods causes pollution, which damages our environment.

- It is unnecessary to import food from Africa. We don't need to eat bananas and pineapples that have to travel so far to get to us; we will be just as healthy if we eat apples or pears, which are grown locally.

- Flying foods from Africa keeps the fruits and vegetables fresh. They retain more of their nutrients, which is good for us. But flying causes more pollution than other forms of transport.

- Supermarkets demand high quality food but pay farmers the lowest price they can. Many farmers in the UK and Africa find it difficult to continue to produce food.

- Many African farmers only receive a very small percentage of the amount we pay for the food. The rest goes on the cost of transport and processing the food.

Activity Sheet 5 requires students to identify reasons for buying UK and African produce.

KS3 GEOGRAPHY TEACHERS' TOOLKIT

LESSON 4:
What can we learn about a place from its shopping facilities??

Key questions
- How do shopping facilities affect people's daily lives in Malawi?

Key words
- maize
- mud hut
- shopping habits

Resources
- Information Sheet 2
- Figures 17-22 from CD
- Activity Sheet 6
- Information Sheet 5
- Activity Sheet 7

Learning objectives
- To develop students' geographical imaginations of rural Africa
- To use maps to understand the elements of daily life in an African village.

Assessment opportunities
- Students complete the map exercise based on Chinamwali village
- Students complete table outlining impacts of possible changes.

Starter
Ask students to consider how they shop by discussing the following questions:
- Where do you shop for food?
- How often do you/your family buy food? Why?
- Do you grow any fruit and vegetables in your garden? Why?
- Where do you/your family buy clothes?
- How much money do you/your family spend on buying clothes?
- Do you ever make your own clothes? Why?
- What would other people learn about us from the way we shop?

Main teaching and learning phase
Show students where Chinamwali is on the overview map of Africa (Information Sheet 2). Give out Activity Sheet 6 – a map of Chinamwali village. Show the photos of Chinamwali village (Figures 17-22) either on an interactive whiteboard or as print copies. Students mark on the map where they think each photo was taken.

This lesson is based on my personal experience of teaching in Chinamwali Private Secondary School. Flora and Kondwani are two students I taught when in Malawi. A private school in Malawi is one where students have to pay school fees to attend. Government schools, while free to attend, only provide school places for a very small percentage of Malawi's children.

KS3 GEOGRAPHY TEACHERS' TOOLKIT

Photos: Emma Cook

Give out Information Sheet 5. Students read through the statements and decide the most likely location on the map for each statement. They mark the number that corresponds to each statement on the map. For example, they will write a 1 on the map where they think statement 1 will take place.

Give out Activity Sheet 7. Students consider what impacts certain events would have on people's daily lives and shopping habits. They write their ideas into the right hand column of the table.

> What if…? or What might…? questions are higher order questions that require students to think more deeply than straightforward Where? What? or Why? questions. Here students have to think about the factors leading to change in an African village.

Plenary/review

Conduct a class discussion. Ask the following questions:
- What can we learn about a place from its shopping facilities?
- How different are people's daily lives and shopping habits from yours?
- How would not having a fridge affect your shopping habits?
- How similar are Kondwani and Flora's lives?
- How different are Kondwani and Flora's lives?
- Why do you think meat is only eaten on special occasions?

Set the homework task for lesson 5. See next lesson plan for details.

23

KS3 GEOGRAPHY TEACHERS' TOOLKIT

LESSON 5:
How does football connect us to Africa?

Key questions
- How does football connect us to Africa?

Key words
- migration
- emigration
- immigration

Resources
- Information Sheet 2
- Information Sheet 6
- Information Sheet 7
- Activity Sheet 8

Learning objectives
- To analyse and evaluate evidence to make decisions
- To be able to understand and empathise with others' lives.

Assessment opportunities
- Students write a letter giving advice.

Prior to the lesson
As a homework task set the previous lesson, students research which African footballers play in British clubs, and which African country they are from.

Starter
Ask students to share with the class their results from the homework task to research which African footballers play in British clubs. Make a list on the whiteboard. Students then shade the countries where these African footballers come from on Activity Sheet 8.

> Footballers come and footballers go – none more quickly than overseas players. This is a lesson you need to update periodically to convince your students you've got your eye on the ball!

Main teaching and learning phase
Show students the location of the Ivory Coast on Information Sheet 2.

Give out Information Sheet 6. As a class, read the letter together, pausing to discuss what the advice should be.

Students then discuss in pairs how they would respond to this letter and what reasons they would give for this with reference to the text.

Students then write a letter in response to George, giving him advice on whether he should take the contract or not. For higher-ability students, give out Information Sheet 7 to help with this task.

> The letter to Aunt Grace sets up a classic moral dilemma. The moral arguments for each course of action are finely balanced. Students are likely to have their own opinions, but encourage them to make their judgement based solely on the evidence they are given.

Plenary/review
For this plenary, invite a colleague into your class, or possibly a student from another class. Read George's letter to them and ask them initially what they would do if they were George. Then invite two students to read their letters giving Aunt Grace's advice – one in favour of going to Europe, the other against. What would they do if they were George? Which advice did they find more convincing? What were the most important arguments? Ask the rest of the class for their views.

Photo: Henrik Hartmann/Morguefile

24

KS3 GEOGRAPHY TEACHERS' TOOLKIT

KS3 GEOGRAPHY TEACHERS' TOOLKIT: INTO AFRICA

LESSON 5: Information Sheet 6

PO Box 234
Abidjan
Ivory Coast
Africa

Dear Aunt Grace

Hello! How are you? Everyone here is fine but mum is finding things hard. Now Margaret, my newborn sister, has arrived, there are nine of us living in our two-roomed house. Sometimes there is not enough to eat and I only have one meal a day. But still, we get by.

Anyway, I wanted to ask your advice, Auntie, as you always know what is best for me. As you know, my friends and I love playing football and I am really good. A year ago I was picked to play for a football academy that is run by a rich Lebanese businessman. He goes to Europe all the time and takes African players with him that he says are making lots and lots of money and becoming very famous. The football academy that I play for is really good. Do you remember near us there was wasteland with the motorway on one side and a rubbish tip on the other? Well that's where our academy is! It is great to have been chosen to play for this academy but there are problems for me. Mum and Dad don't have enough money to buy me football boots so I have to play barefoot and the pitch is often covered in broken glass and tin cans, which cut my feet if I tread on them.

Anyway, the other day a talent scout came to the club and said that a European club wants to sign me up! He has got to talk to my Lebanese coach to agree a price. It's really exciting but I am not sure whether I should take up this offer or not? Would you be able to give me your advice?

If it all worked out, it could be a really good opportunity for our family to be rich and escape from this difficult life. Just think, I could be as successful as Jay-Jay Okocho, Michael Essien, Samuel Eto'o, or Didier Drogba! Wow! Did you know that Jay-Jay Okocho started a bit like me? I will tell you his story as this may help you to give me advice on whether to accept his offer.

He grew up in Nigeria in a small town and played football in the street. When he was 13 he played for his school team and after secondary school, he was lucky enough to be able to go on a trip to Germany to stay with a friend of his brother's who played for a third division team in Germany. The manager let him train with them for two weeks, and after the second day's training they thought he was really good and so offered him a two-week trial. Then the club registered him, and his football career began. He kept becoming more and more successful and now he has played in three World Cups, has won BBC African Footballer of the Year twice, and is captain of Nigeria. Could this be me, Auntie?

And do you remember our neighbour Traore? He has recently signed for the Norwegian club Rosenborg and earns $8000 a month. Just think what our family could do with $8000! So much money! Mum is very proud of me and quite keen for me to go, although I know she would worry about me being so far away.

On the other hand I have heard stories that some of these talent scouts are not honest people. My friend told me of a boy, who lived in a nearby village, who was playing for a different football academy. An agent spotted him and offered him a contract to play in Europe for a successful club. It was his dream to play in Europe so he was very happy. Apparently, he couldn't read very well and so didn't read the contract that was given to him. He went to France and ended up playing for a third division club. His agent received all the money and he didn't have enough money to pay for some of the basic things like rent and food. He couldn't send any money home to his family. His contract ended last month and he didn't have enough money to stay, so is now back home in the Ivory Coast looking for a club to sign him. Auntie – imagine – life was worse for them in Europe than here at home.

Another boy in our village was offered a contract to play for a club in Europe and then was dropped by the club soon after he arrived. He was never paid and is now living illegally in the country. He is scared that he will be arrested at any time.

This decision is such a big one and I am not sure what to do. What do you think, Auntie? Should I go to Europe and hope that the contract is good and that I become a successful footballer? Or should I stay in the Ivory Coast, in case the contract is not a good one, and hope that another opportunity comes along which will be good for me?

Write soon and let me know what you think!

Love George

Information Sheet 6: George's letter to Aunt Grace.

25

KS3 GEOGRAPHY TEACHERS' TOOLKIT

LESSON 6:

What are the likely impacts of the 2010 World Cup on South Africa?

Key question
- What are the likely impacts of the 2010 World Cup on South Africa?

Key words
- tourism
- shanty town
- social
- environmental
- economic

Resources
- Information Sheet 2
- Information Sheet 8
- Activity Sheet 9
- Figure 23 from CD
- Large pieces of sugar paper
- Colouring pencils

Learning objectives
- To explore the likely impact of the 2010 World Cup on South Africa
- To analyse and evaluate evidence to draw and justify conclusions.

Assessment opportunities
- Students carry out a cost-benefit analysis justifying their decisions in pairs and with the teacher
- Students write about the likely impacts of the 2010 Fifa World Cup.

Starter
Show students the location of South Africa on the map on Information Sheet 2. Students read Information Sheet 8, either on an interactive whiteboard or as a hand-out. They identify the key elements and aims of the 2010 World Cup and come up with their own slogan or logo for it.

Main teaching and learning phase
Cut out the statements in Activity Sheet 9 and give them to the students. In pairs, students carry out a cost-benefit analysis. They sort the statements into two piles: likely benefits of hosting the World Cup and costs (problems) of hosting the World Cup. They shade in the cards showing benefits in one colour and the problems in another colour. They will probably have more benefits than costs.

Show the students Figure 23 and ask them to copy the diagram onto a large piece of sugar paper. They try to divide the cards into social, economic and environmental impacts and place them onto the correct section of the diagram. Point out to students that some cards will fit into more than one section.

> At the time of writing, the World Cup had not taken place. After the event has happened, there is likely to be much evaluation of its success. It would be interesting to compare the likely impacts with the actual impacts. Some of the web links at the end of the unit would be a useful starting point for this.

> You may need to explain the terms, 'social', 'economic' and 'environmental', or students could use the glossary. It is useful for students to build up their own glossary of geographical vocabulary.

26

KS3 GEOGRAPHY TEACHERS' TOOLKIT

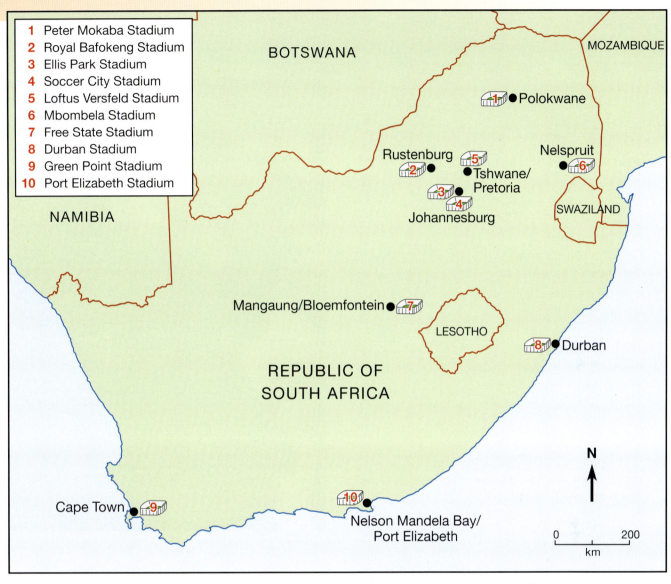

1 Peter Mokaba Stadium
2 Royal Bafokeng Stadium
3 Ellis Park Stadium
4 Soccer City Stadium
5 Loftus Versfeld Stadium
6 Mbombela Stadium
7 Free State Stadium
8 Durban Stadium
9 Green Point Stadium
10 Port Elizabeth Stadium

Information Sheet 8 shows the location of the stadia for the 2010 World Cup.

Students write answers to the following questions:
- What are the main costs of hosting the 2010 Fifa World Cup?
- Are the main costs social, economic or environmental?
- What are the main benefits of hosting the 2010 Fifa World Cup?
- Are the main benefits social, economic or environmental?
- Are there more benefits than costs?
- Should the 2010 Fifa World Cup be held in South Africa?

Plenary/review

Conduct a class discussion to give feedback on the students' answers to the questions above.

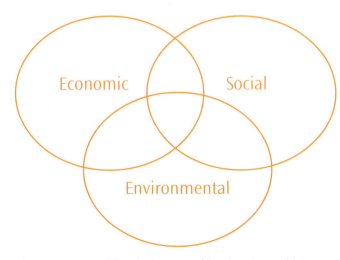

Figure 23: Categorising the impacts of hosting the World Cup.

27

KS3 GEOGRAPHY TEACHERS' TOOLKIT

LESSON 7:
How do mobile phones connect us to Africa?

Key questions
- How do mobile phones connect us to Africa?

Key words
- multinational
- coltan

Resources
- Information Sheet 2
- Figures 24 and 25 from CD
- Information Sheet 9
- Information Sheet 10
- Activity Sheet 10

Learning objectives
- To analyse and evaluate evidence to draw and justify conclusions
- To consider how our decisions could affect people in Africa.

Assessment opportunities
- Students complete a table on what should be done about coltan mining.

Starter
Give students a copy of Figures 24 and 25 (or show them on an interactive whiteboard). Ask students if they can think of any way that these two people are linked. It is likely that they will not have many ideas! However, encourage them to be imaginative and, in pairs, to make up a story that links the two people.

> Mysteries are a good way to get students thinking in geography. Asking them to make up their own story, however ridiculous it is, will help to increase the intrigue and suspense when the real connection is gradually revealed.

Figure 24: How is this woman in the UK linked to Africa?

Show students the location of the Democratic Republic of Congo on the overview map of Africa (Information Sheet 2).

Tell the class that they are going to find out how the two people in Figures 24 and 25 are linked. Give students a copy of Information Sheet 9, cut into cards, or show the paragraphs one at a time on the interactive whiteboard. Starting with the first card, read out the information and then ask students if they can think of any way that the two people are linked. Continue to read out the next card and so on until they get to the seventh card, asking students after every card if they can link the two people. It will probably not be until then that students can link the two!

KS3 GEOGRAPHY TEACHERS' TOOLKIT

Figure 25: How are these miners in the Democratic Republic of Congo linked to the UK?

In small groups, students consider the following questions and then they feed back their ideas to the class as a whole:
- Did these men choose to become coltan miners?
- How would living in a war zone affect these men's families?
- What are the good things about being a coltan miner?
- Are there any bad things about being a coltan miner?
- What difficulties do you think these families face?

Give out Information Sheet 10, which investigates whether anything should be done about coltan mining, and Activity Sheet 10. Make clear to students that this is not an easy situation to resolve. Students read through each option on Information Sheet 10 and then write down in the table on Activity Sheet 10 the good things and problems with each option.

Plenary/review
In pairs, students decide which of the options outlined in Information Sheet 10 would be the best for each of the following:
- The Gorillas of Kahuzi Biega National Park
- The rainforest in and around Kahuzi Biega National Park
- The coltan miners and their families
- The mobile phone companies.

Students feed back their ideas to the whole class.

Set the homework task for the next lesson. See next lesson plan for details.

29

KS3 GEOGRAPHY TEACHERS' TOOLKIT

LESSON 8:

How have mobile phones been changing lives in Nigeria and the UK?

Key questions
- How have mobile phones been changing lives in Nigeria and in the UK?

Key words
- informal sector
- fixed-line telephone
- mobile phone
- rural
- urban

Resources
- Information Sheet 2
- Figure 26 from CD
- Activity Sheet 11 (completed as homework prior to the lesson)
- Information Sheet 11

Learning objectives
- To understand how places are changing and the implications of this change for people
- To appreciate the similarities and differences between the UK and Nigeria.

Assessment opportunities
- Students complete a table to compare changing mobile phone use in the UK and Nigeria.

Prior to the lesson
As a homework task set the previous lesson, students consider how mobile phones have been changing people's lives in the UK. They complete the first column of the table on Activity Sheet 11 at home with an adult. The second column should be left blank.

Starter
In pairs in class, students compare their answers on Activity Sheet 11 to see how their experience of changing technology is similar or different. Students share their findings with the whole class.

Main teaching and learning phase
Show students the location of Nigeria on the overview map of Africa (Information Sheet 2).

Read through Information Sheet 11 with the students, either on an interactive whiteboard or as a handout, and show Figure 26. Students will learn about how mobile phones have changed people's lives in Nigeria. They use this information to complete the second column on Activity Sheet 11.

Students discuss the following questions in pairs:
- Have the changes been the same in the UK and Nigeria?
- Do people use mobile phones for different things in Nigeria and the UK?
- Are there any differences in mobile phone use between rural and urban areas in the UK?
- Are there any differences in mobile phone use between rural and urban areas in Nigeria?
- How important are mobile phones for young people in Nigeria and the UK?
- How important are mobile phones for adults and business people in Nigeria and the UK?
- Is it likely that everyone in Nigeria will have a mobile phone in ten years time?
- Are mobile phones more important for people in Nigeria than in the UK?
- How different might things be in ten years' time in Nigeria and the UK?

> You could use all of these questions or select from the list, according to the time available and the students you teach. They are intended to take students beyond mere comprehension of what they have read about Nigeria, to compare Nigeria and the UK.

Plenary
In pairs, students prepare a brief talk or act out a scene to show how they think things will be different in ten years' time either in the UK or Nigeria. Invite students to present their talk or their scene to the whole class.

KS3 GEOGRAPHY TEACHERS' TOOLKIT

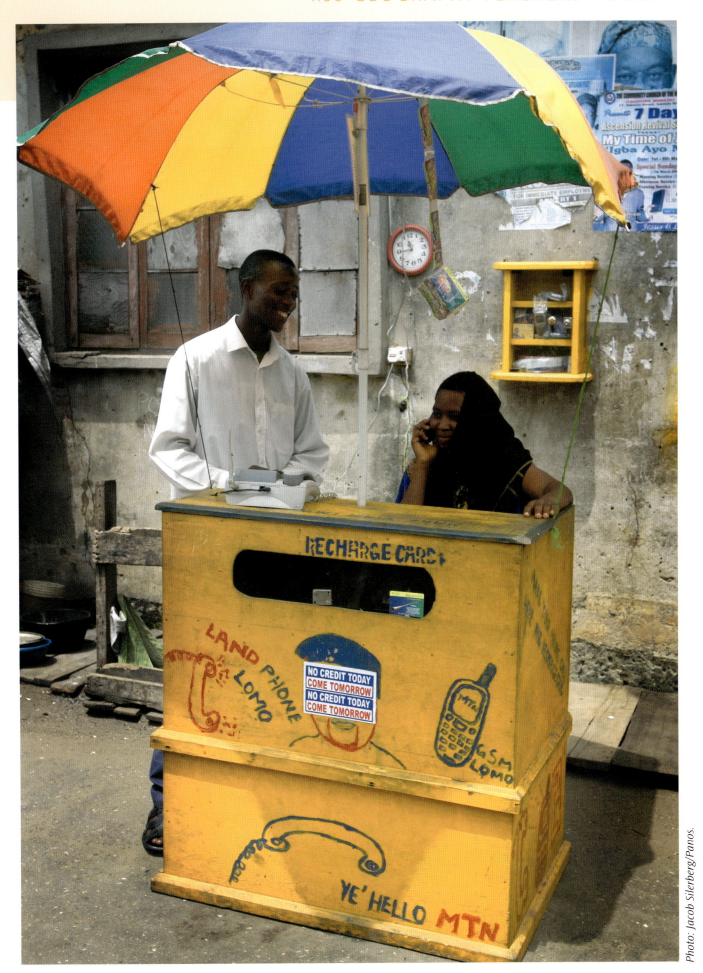

Figure 26: A woman operates a booth selling mobile phone calls in Lagos, Nigeria.

KS3 GEOGRAPHY TEACHERS' TOOLKIT

LESSON 9:
How does Comic Relief connect us to Africa?

Key question
- How does Comic Relief connect us to Africa?

Key word
- shanty town

Resources
- Information Sheet 2
- Comic Relief website (www.rednoseday.com)
- Information Sheet 12
- Activity Sheet 12
- Information Sheet 13
- Card for photocopying Activity Sheet 12
- Scissors and sticky tape

Learning objectives
- To develop students' geographical imaginations of urban Africa
- To interpret place and space through creating a model of a shanty town home.

Assessment opportunities
- Students complete a scale model of David's home
- Students analyse aspects of David's life.

Starter
Tell the class that this lesson is going to explore Comic Relief. Elicit from students what they think happens when money is donated to Comic Relief and the reasons why we donate money. You could then show a video clip featuring Ant and Dec from the Comic Relief website. Students take notes about problems for people living in Kibera whilst watching the video. They feedback their ideas after the video.

> 60% of the money raised by Comic Relief helps to give people living in grinding poverty across Africa a better chance of life. 40% helps disadvantaged people and communities across the UK turn their lives around.

Main teaching and learning phase
Show students where Kibera is on the overview map of Africa (Information Sheet 2). Students are going to carry out an activity which aims to help them to empathise with a Kiberan family. Divide the class into pairs and give out Information Sheet 12 or put the information on an interactive whiteboard. Conduct a brief discussion to compare David's life with ours.

Give out Activity Sheet 12 which has the templates for David's home, a base map, furniture, and models of David's family. Information Sheet 13 has instructions on how to carry out the activity. Divide the class into pairs and explain that they are going to make a scale model of David's family's house. You can read out the instructions or the students can read them in their pairs.

KS3 GEOGRAPHY TEACHERS' TOOLKIT

Photo: Margaret Mackintosh.

When they have completed the model, students consider the following questions. They can discuss them in their pairs then write down their answers:
- How much space does the family have?
- What problems would this lead to?
- What health problems might the family face?
- What are the good things in David's life?
- How does David's home compare to your home?
- Did anything surprise you when you carried out this activity?

> Some students are kinaesthetic learners – they learn through doing physical activity. Making a shanty home is likely to be a memorable learning experience for these students.

Information Sheet 12 profiles David's life in Kibera, Kenya.

Plenary

Ask students to place their homes together on one desk in the classroom. They have created their own shanty town! Just for fun, they could vote on the best-made home. What problems did they find in building their home? Would they face similar problems if they were building a real home? How do they think they would survive living in Kibera?

33

KS3 GEOGRAPHY TEACHERS' TOOLKIT

LESSON 10:

How has Comic Relief helped to change lives in Kibera?

Key question

- How has Comic Relief helped to change lives in Kibera?

Key words

- charcoal
- sewage

Resources

- Information Sheet 12
- Information Sheet 14
- Information Sheet 15

Learning objectives

- To analyse and evaluate evidence to draw and justify conclusions
- To understand how places are changing and the implications of this change for people.

Assessment opportunities

- Students carry out hot-seating activity
- Students describe ways that Kicoshep is helping to improve lives.

Starter

Students imagine that that they are David, the young person introduced in lesson 9 (see Information Sheet 12). Tell them that three months ago David picked up a leaflet about the Kicoshep youth centre and has been going there regularly ever since. The Kicoshep youth centre is funded in part by Comic Relief money. Divide the class into pairs and give them a copy of the Kicoshep leaflet (Information Sheet 14). They discuss and write down how they think Kicoshep's youth centre can help David improve his life.

Main teaching and learning phase

Keeping the students in pairs set up a hot-seating activity.

One of the pair is to imagine they are a newspaper journalist who is writing an article for the local paper about the Kicoshep youth centre. Give these students the interviewer's brief (Information Sheet 15) or encourage them to think of their own questions. The other student in the pair is to imagine they are David, who has been going to the youth centre for three months.

You could start by modelling an interview, asking one or two of the questions from the journalist's brief (see below) to one of the students playing David. It would be a good idea for each person to have a copy of Information Sheet 14. Once students have grasped the idea, they carry out interviews in their pairs.

> Hot-seating is a type of role-play activity that helps to develop students' speaking and listening skills. In this example, the interviewer can frame their own questions while the interviewee empathises with someone living in Kibera. Students can take turns in both roles.

- What problems do you face living in Kibera?
- Do you go to school?
- How did you find out about the Kicoshep youth centre?
- How long have you been going to the Kicoshep youth centre?
- How often do you go there?
- What do you do when you go to the youth centre?
- How has the youth centre helped improve your life?
- What is the best thing about the Kicoshep youth centre?
- Are there any bad things about the Kicoshep youth centre?
- What other projects might also help people living in Kibera?

34

KS3 GEOGRAPHY TEACHERS' TOOLKIT

Invite students to show their interviews to the class. Encourage other students to comment critically on the questions and answers they hear.

Students then rewrite the interview as a newspaper article. They can use some of the following questions as a guide to structure their writing:

- What are the main ways that Kicoshep youth centre is helping young people living in Kibera?
- How does the Kicoshep youth centre compare with a youth centre in your area?
- Is running the Kicoshep youth centre a good way to spend Comic Relief money?
- What other projects might help people living in Kibera? (Students could research other projects that are taking place.)

We often ask students to do things that we would not want to do ourselves. Hot-seating may be one of those things! However, modelling the activity will alert you to potential problems the students might face and, hopefully, inspire them to emulate your example.

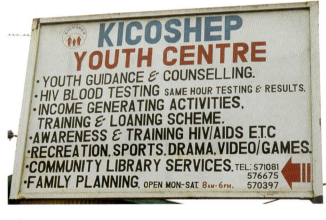

Photos: Sarah Maude

Plenary

Ask students to think back over all the work they have done in this unit and to consider the connections that exist between the UK and Africa. They write a list of as many ways they can think of that the UK and Africa are connected. They may think of others not mentioned in the unit, e.g. migration. Students consider whether these connections are good for the UK and Africa, or what the problems of being connected are.

Thanks to Sarah Maude for the information about Kicoshep and Kibera.

35

KS3 GEOGRAPHY TEACHERS' TOOLKIT

4: GLOSSARY

charcoal – fuel made from wood used for cooking

coltan – a mineral used in mobile phones that prolongs the life of the battery

continent – a large continuous land mass comprising many countries

country – an area that has its own government

development – industrialisation or economic advancement

economic – to do with business and related activities that are designed to make money

emigration – the movement of people from a country

environmental – to do with the natural and artificial world around us

export – take something out of a country, probably to be sold

fixed-line telephone – telephone that connects via cables

gross domestic product (GDP) – the total value of goods produced and services provided in a country in one year

immigration – the movement of people into a country

import – bring something into a country, probably to be sold

informal sector – an area of the economy which is unregulated and involves individuals working for themselves, not paying taxes or necessarily obeying employment law

LEDC – less economically developed country

maize – corn crop that is the staple crop in Africa

MEDC – more economically developed country

migration – the movement of people

mobile phone – telephone that connects through the air to radio masts

mud hut – traditional house found in Africa typically made of wood, sticks and a thatched roof

multinational – a large company with interests in several countries

rural – in the countryside

sewage – domestic waste including human waste

shanty town – a whole area, usually around a city, of makeshift housing made from found objects

shopping habits – the way in which people shop, e.g. they may shop daily or once a week

social – things that are to do with people and how people get on with each other

tourism – an industry involved in the organisation and operation of holidays

tourist – a person who is on holiday

urban – a built up area such as a town or city

KS3 GEOGRAPHY TEACHERS' TOOLKIT

5: LINKS FOR FURTHER IDEAS AND RESOURCES

Bibliography

Adelaja, A. (2007) *Biofuels could soon be powering mobile phone networks*. www.scidev.net (viewed 16/2/2007).

Ali, J.(2005) *Africa Lives: Jay-Jay Okocha*. www.bbc.co.uk/manchester/content/articles/2005/07/04/africa_okocha_040705_feature.shtml (viewed 25/9/2007).

Bell, D. (2005) 'The value and importance of geography', *Teaching Geography*, 30, 1, pp. 12-13.

Blunt, E. (2006) *Ringing in changes in Nigeria*. www.bbc.co.uk (viewed 18/3/2006).

Brazier, C. (1995) 'Across the great divide', *New Internationalist*, 268, pp. 23-5.

Brooks, C. and Morgan, A. (2006) *Theory into Practice: Cases and Places*. Sheffield: Geographical Association.

Butler, R. (2005) *Cell phones may help 'save' Africa*. www.mongabay.com (viewed 11/7/2005).

Castle, S., Smith, A.D. and Rundle, L. (2000) *Inquiry into 'slave trade' in African footballers*. http://news.independent.co.uk/europe/article152253.ece (viewed 25/9/2007).

Commission for Africa (2005) *Our Common Interest*. Glasgow: DFID Public Enquiry Point.

DfES/QCA (2007) *Geography: Programme of study for key stage 3*. London: DfES/QCA.

Diamond, J. (2005) 'The Shape of Africa', *National Geographic*, September, 208, 3.

Durbin, C. (2006) 'Media literacy and geographical imaginations' in Balderstone, D. (ed) *Secondary Geography Handbook*. Sheffield: Geographical Association.

Geldof, B. (2005) *Geldof in Africa*. London: Random House.

Gray, V. (2006) *The un-wired continent: Africa's mobile success story*. www.itu.int/ITU-D/ict/statistics/at_glance/Africa_EE2006_e.pdf (viewed 25/9/2007).

Hickman, M. (2007) *The Big Question: Should we buy produce that has been flown in from abroad?* http://news.independent.co.uk/uk/this_britain/article2594124.ece (viewed 25/9/2007).

Hill, J. and Woodward, W. (2005) 'Globalisation and Culture: A case study of two subterranean communities in southern Tunisia', *Geography*, 90, 1, pp. 42-53.

Joseph, J. (2000) 'Why a black perspective on development education?', *The Development Education Journal*, 6, pp. 3-6.

Kapuscinski, R. (2001) *The Shadow of the Sun*. London: Penguin.

Kuada, J. and Chachah, Y. (1999) *Ghana: Understanding the people and their culture*. Accra: Woell Publishing Services.

Lambert, D., Martin, F. and Swift, D. (2005) 'GeoVisions: Past, present and future', *Teaching Geography*, 30, 1, pp. 12-13.

Laurance, J. (2005) *Whole nations at risk from virus that has bred a generation of orphans*. http://news.independent.co.uk/world/africa/article14742.ece (viewed 25/9/2007).

Ledge, F. (2002) *Nigeria's digital revolution*. www.bbc.co.uk (viewed 11/7/2002).

Lockwood, M. (2005) *The Agenda for International Action on Poverty in Africa*. Warwickshire: ITDG Publishing.

McDougall, D. *Inside the football factories that feed the beautiful game*. http://observer.guardian.co.uk/world/story/0,,2099499,00.html (viewed 25/9/2007).

Obayiuwana, O. (2001) *African fortune-seekers struggle abroad*. www.bbc.co.uk (viewed 6/4/2001).

Okocha, J.(2005) *Jay-Jay's football journey*. http://news.bbc.co.uk/sportacademy/hi/sa/football/features/newsid_3720000/3720830.stm (viewed 25/9/2007).

Okocha, J. (2005) *Jay-Jay: My lucky break*. http://news.bbc.co.uk/sportacademy/hi/sa/football/features/newsid_3721000/3721254.stm (viewed 25/9/2007).

Morris, P. and Jacobs, D. (2005) *The Rough Guide to Tunisia*. London: Rough Guide Ltd.

Reader, J. (2001) *National Geographic: Africa*. Westchester, OH: National Geographic.

Rice, X. (2007) *Ready or not*. http://football.guardian.co.uk/News_Story/0,,2091484,00.html (viewed 25/9/2007).

Sawano, N. (2001) *In a Village Far, Far Away, Star Wars Stirs Debate*. www.csmonitor.com/2001/0809/p7s2-woaf.html (viewed 25/9/2007).

Scott, N., Batchelor, S., Ridley, J. and Jorgensen. B. (2004) *The impact of mobile phones in Africa*. www.commissionforafrica.org/french/report/background/scott_et_al_background.pdf (viewed 25/9/2007).

Sopel, J. (2000) *Africa's football 'slave' trade*. http://news.bbc.co.uk/1/hi/world/europe/639390.stm (viewed 25.9.2007).

Taylor, L. (2005) 'Place: An exploration', *Teaching Geography*, 30, 1, pp. 14-17.

Thorton, G. (2007) *2010 Soccer World Cup facts you should know*. http://www.tourismcapetown.co.za/xxl/_lang/en/_site/visit-travel/_area/westerncape/_subArea/355754/_subArea2//_subArea3//_articleId/759684/index.html#2010soccerworld (viewed 25/9/2007).

Wisner, B., Toulmin, C. and Chitiga, R. (2005) *Towards a new map of Africa*. London: Earthscan.

Wellsted, E. (2006) 'Understanding distant places' in Balderstone, D. (ed) *Secondary Geography Handbook*. Sheffield: Geographical Association.

www.bbc.co.uk (2005) *Local food 'greener than organic'*. http://news.bbc.co.uk/1/hi/sci/tech/4312591.stm (viewed 25/9/2007).

www.bbc.co.uk (2006) *FifPro to tackle African exodus.*
http://news.bbc.co.uk/sport1/hi/football/africa/6176964.
stm (viewed 25/9/2007).

Zuckerman, E. (2005) *Africa Calling - SND MNY 2 YR MBL.*
www.worldchanging.com/archives/003423.html (viewed
25/9/2007).

Websites

Holidays

Tunisia
www.tunisia.com
www.wordtravels.com/Travelguide/Countries/Tunisia/Photos
www.vakantieboeken.nl

Egypt
www.1uptravel.com
www.guardians.net
www.goegypt.org

Lalibela
www.nilefall.com
www.ethioembassy.org.uk
www.gojoethiopiatravel.com

Bwindi National Park
www.ecoafrica.com
www.africanpearlsafaris.com
www.unesco.org

Mount Kilimanjaro
www.junglephotos.com
www.mountkenyaexpeditions.com
www.explore.co.uk
www.panoramaholidays.co.uk
www.safari.co.uk
www.exodus.co.uk
www.truckafrica.com

Matmata
www.gonomad.com
www.lexicorient.com
www.tunisia.com
www.backpackerinfo.net

Shopping
www.co-opfairtrade.co.uk
www.fairtrade.org.uk
www.tesco.com/regionalsourcing
www.sainsburys.co.uk/food/foodandfeatures/sainsburysandfood/fairtrade
www.waitrose.com/food/originofourfood
www.redtractor.org.uk
www.riverford.co.uk
www.fieldfare-organics.com/Fresh_Produce/Vegetables/

Football
www.unwto.org
www.fifa.com
www.capegateway.gov.za
www.capetown.gov.za
www.bbc.co.uk

Mobile phones
www.wwf.org.uk
www.seeingisbelieving.com
www.gorillas.org
www.wrm.org.uy
www.zooatlanta.org
www.bbc.co.uk
www.commissionforafrica.org
www.itu.int

Comic Relief
www.rednoseday.com
www.maendeleo-ya-wanawake.org

KS3 GEOGRAPHY TEACHERS' TOOLKIT

6: ASSESSMENT FRAMEWORK:
How are we connected to Africa?

Level 7-8

- Students use atlases and maps of Africa at different scales to fully develop their knowledge and understanding.
- Students can recognise bias and opinion in sources of evidence.

Level 5-6

- Students use atlases and maps of Africa at different scales to develop their knowledge and understanding of Africa

Level 3-4

- Students use atlases and maps of Africa at different scales
- Students recognise the connections between Africa and the UK.
- Students present information and draw simple conclusions.
- Students recognise there are similarities and differences between people, places, environments and cultures.

- Students understand how places are changing and the implications of this change for people

- Students recognise and appreciate the similarities and differences between people, places, environments and cultures.

- Students develop understanding of social, economic and environmental connections between Africa and the UK

- Students develop understanding of social, economic and environmental connections and the significance of interdependence.

- Students present and evaluate information to draw plausible conclusions.

- Students present information in a variety of ways and evaluate it to draw substantial conclusions.

- Students recognise and appreciate the similarities and differences between people, places, environments and cultures and how these shape places.

39

PoS coverage in the *Toolkit* series

KS3 GEOGRAPHY TEACHERS' TOOLKIT

		Into Africa	Rise and Rise of China	British or European?	Look at it this way	Water works	Thorny issue	Faster, higher, stronger	Changing my world	Moving stories	Future floods
KEY CONCEPTS	Place	✓	✓	✓	★	★	★	✓	★	★	✓
	Space	★	★	★	✓	✓	★	✓	★	✓	
	Scale	★	★	★	★	★	★	★	✓	★	★
	Interdependence	✓	✓	★		★	✓		★	★	
	Physical human process		★		✓	★	✓	✓	✓		★
	Environmental interaction	★	✓		✓	✓		★	✓		✓
	Diversity	✓		✓	★			★	★	✓	
KEY PROCESSES	Enquiry	✓	✓	✓	✓	✓	✓	✓	✓	✓	✓
	Fieldwork				★						✓
	Graphicacy	★	★	✓	★	★		★	★	✓	✓
	Communication	★			★	★	★	✓	★	★	★
RANGE AND CONTENT	Variety of scale	★		★		★		★	✓	★	
	Location	★	★	✓	★						★
	Aspects of UK			✓	★			✓	★	✓	✓
	Parts of the world	✓	✓	✓		✓	✓		★		
	Physical geography				✓	★	★				★
	Human geography	✓	★	★					★	✓	
	People-environment	★	✓		✓	✓	★	★	✓		✓
CURRICULUM OPPORTUNITIES	Personal experience	★		✓	★	★	★		★	★	
	Contemporary context	✓	✓	★	★	★	★	✓	★	★	★
	Enquiry approaches	★	★	★	★	★	✓	★	★	★	★
	Maps & GIS	★	★	★	★	★	★	★	★	★	✓
	Fieldwork				★						✓
	Responsible action	★		✓		★	✓	★	✓		
	Issues in the news	★	✓	★	★	✓	★	✓	✓	✓	✓
	Use of ICT				✓		★	★	★		★
	Curriculum links			★	★	★	★	★		✓	

KEY: ✓ major focus/fully developed   ★ additional aspect